Wacky Plant Cycles

by Valerie Wyatt
illustrated by Lilith Jones

MONDO

For my wacky friend, Farns—V.W.

For the dear family and beloved memory of Mary E. Richard—L.J.

Photograph Credits: Dr. J. Burgess/Photo Researchers, Inc: p. 7; © G. Büttner/Naturbild/OKAPIA/Photo Researchers, Inc: p. 8 (top); © Dan Suzio/Photo Researchers, Inc: p. 8 (bottom); © Jerome Wexler/Photo Researchers, Inc: p. 10 (left); p. 15 (right); Dr. Wm. M. Harlow/Photo Researchers, Inc: p. 10 (right); © Cabisco/Visuals Unlimited: p. 11; © Stan Flegler/Visuals Unlimited: p. 12 (top); © Reed S. Beaman/Bio-Photo Services, Inc: p. 12 (bottom); © Ken Brate/Photo Researchers, Inc: p. 13; © E. R. Degginger/Photo Researchers, Inc: p. 15 (left); © James Welgos/ National Audubon Society/Photo Researchers, Inc: p. 15 (middle); © Ray Simons/Photo Researchers, Inc: p. 16 (top); © Walt Anderson/Visuals Unlimited: p. 16 (bottom); © Jim Steinberg/Photo Researchers, Inc: p. 18; © Jeff Lepore/Photo Researchers, Inc: p. 19; © Rod Planck/Photo Researchers, Inc: p. 20; © David Sieren/Visuals Unlimited: p. 21; © Wally Eberhart/Visuals Unlimited: p. 23.

The author and the publisher gratefully acknowledge Dr. Richard Hebda, Botany Department, Royal British Columbia Museum, for his assistance.

The editor thanks Nancy Lindenauer, principal, The Searingtown School, Albertson, N.Y., for her assistance.

The illustrations for this book were done in watercolor and pen and ink.
The text type for this book is Journal Text.

For information contact:
MONDO Publishing
980 Avenue of the Americas
New York, NY 10018
MONDO is a registered trademark of Mondo Publishing
Visit our website at www.mondopub.com

Printed in China
07 08 09 10 11 12   9 8 7 6 5 4

Designed by Edward Miller

ISBN 1-57255-795-8

Library of Congress Cataloging-in-Publication Data

Wyatt, Valerie.
   Wacky plant cycles / by Valerie Wyatt ; illustrated by Lilith Jones.
      p. cm.
   ISBN 1-57255-795-8 (pbk.)
1. Plant life cycles--Juvenile literature. 2. Plants--Juvenile literature. [1. Plants.] I.
Jones, Lilith. II. Title.

QK49 .W97 2000
571.8o2--dc21
                                     00-042357

CONTENTS

A Plant Puzzle 4

What Is a Life Cycle? 6

A Seed Sprouts 7

A Plant Grows 10

A Flower Blooms 12

A New Seed Forms 14

The Seed Finds a New Home 16

Why Do Plants Have Life Cycles? 18

Different Plant Life Cycles 20

See a Life Cycle 22

Glossary 24

A PLANT PUZZLE

Imagine walking through this forest.
Can you find the following?

- some seeds
- a seed that has just sprouted
- a seedling (young plant)
- a plant with flower buds
- a mature plant with flowers
- a plant with seed pods
- a decaying plant

The plants you see here are at different stages of their **life cycles**.

WHAT IS A LIFE CYCLE?

A plant goes through stages as it grows. These stages are its life cycle.

The cycle begins when a seed falls to the ground. A young plant called a **seedling** sprouts from the seed. It grows into a mature plant. The mature plant produces a **flower**. A new seed forms in the flower. The seed falls to the ground. From seed to plant to seed—the cycle is complete.

The seed falls to the ground.

The seedling sprouts.

Look out below!

The flower produces a seed.

The mature plant produces a flower.

The seedling grows into a mature plant.

A SEED SPROUTS

A **seed** contains a tiny new plant. This plant "sleeps" until it has the right temperature, light, and water. When water weakens the hard outer covering, the tiny new plant begins to swell. It finds an opening and pokes through, like a chick breaking out of an egg. In plants, this is called **germination**.

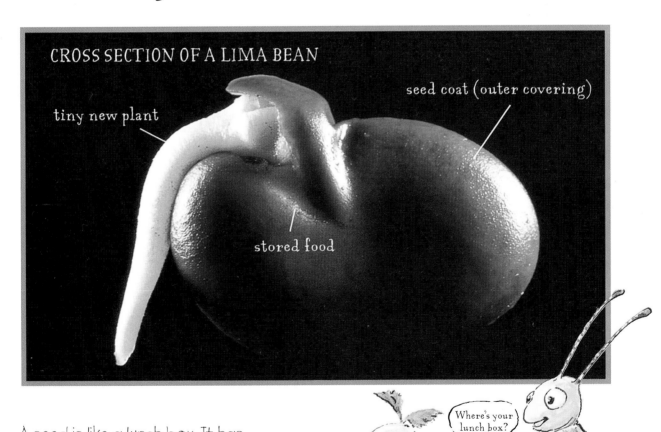

CROSS SECTION OF A LIMA BEAN

tiny new plant

seed coat (outer covering)

stored food

A seed is like a lunch box. It has food for the new plant and its tough outer covering protects the plant from harm.

Where's your lunch box?

Some seeds are smaller than the dot on this "i." But this seed is bigger than a baseball. It is a coconut, the seed of a palm tree.

Many seeds need to be cold before they will germinate. But this jack pine seed likes it hot! It only germinates after it has gone through a forest fire.

Do you like peanut butter sandwiches? Peanuts are actually seeds. So is the grain used to make the bread. How many other seeds can you find in your kitchen?

A PLANT GROWS

The seedling pokes its stem out of the ground and opens its leaves. It needs food to grow. At first it uses food stored in the seed. When that is gone, the young plant makes its own food. How? The plant uses the sun's energy to change carbon dioxide from the air and water into food. This is called **photosynthesis**.

The green coloring in leaves comes from **chlorophyll**. It helps with photosynthesis. In the fall, when there is less sunlight, leaves die and the green color fades away.

leaf

trigger hairs

Like other plants, the Venus's-flytrap can make its own food through photosynthesis. But it also likes an insect snack now and then. When an insect touches one of the trigger hairs on its leaves, the leaves snap shut, trapping the insect inside. Juices in the leaf kill the unlucky insect and digest it.

Bamboo is the fastest growing plant in the world. It can grow 35.4 inches [90 centimeters]—about your height—in just one day.

A FLOWER BLOOMS

When a plant grows up, it produces flowers. Inside each flower there is an **ovary** where new seeds will form. But before this can happen, the **pollen** on the **anthers** must find its way to the **pistil**. This is called **pollination**.

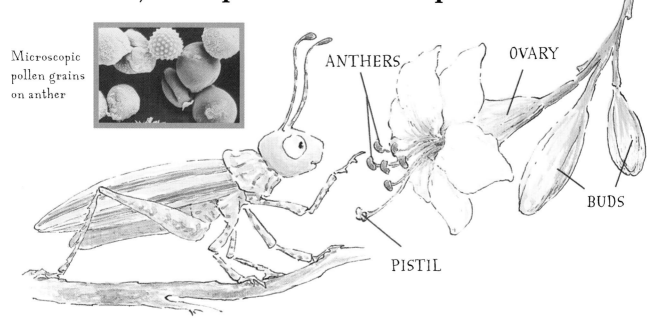

Microscopic pollen grains on anther

ANTHERS

OVARY

BUDS

PISTIL

Flowers look very different, but they all have the same basic parts.

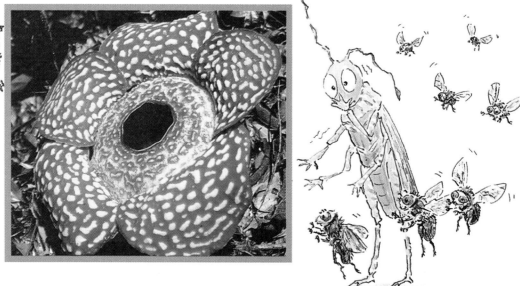

The stinking corpse lily has the world's biggest flower—up to 3 feet [1 meter] across.

The smallest flower blooms on the artillery plant. You could fit eight of its flowers inside this "o."

WACKY!

The flowers on a large purslane plant can produce over a million seeds. Only a few of these seeds will grow into a mature plant.

Flowers that have bright colors and sweet smells attract birds and insects. How are these creatures important to flowers? Turn the page to find out.

A NEW SEED FORMS

Sometimes pollen travels from the anther to the pistil of the same plant. This is called **self-pollination**. Other times, the pollen from the one plant travels to another plant. This is called **cross-pollination**. Once pollen reaches the pistil, a seed can form in the ovary of the flower.

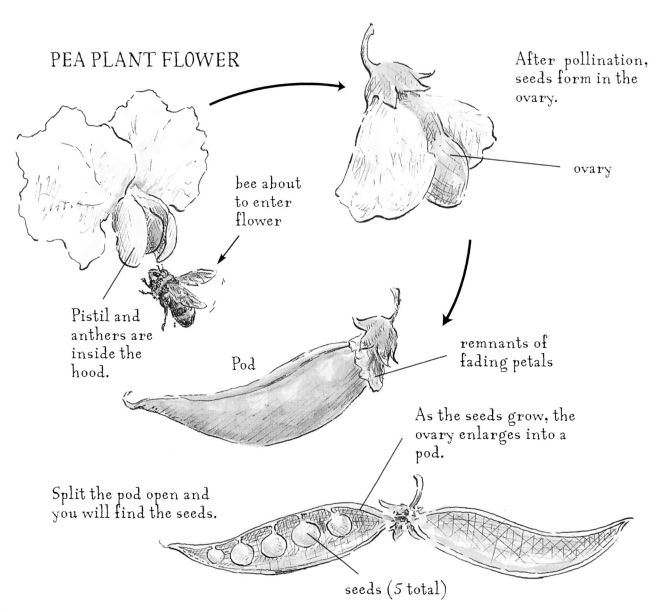

PEA PLANT FLOWER

bee about to enter flower

After pollination, seeds form in the ovary.

ovary

Pistil and anthers are inside the hood.

Pod

remnants of fading petals

As the seeds grow, the ovary enlarges into a pod.

Split the pod open and you will find the seeds.

seeds (5 total)

This hummingbird doesn't know it but it is helping to pollinate a plant. Hummingbirds, insects, and even bats get dusted with pollen as they sip nectar. They carry pollen from one plant to another.

SAGUARO   APPLE   CUCUMBER

The ovaries of many plants grow a thick covering around the seeds. This is called the **fruit** of the plant.

THE SEED FINDS A NEW HOME

A seed must find the right place to germinate. If it falls too close to the parent plant, it may not get the soil, water, and light it needs. So seeds have come up with ways to travel to new homes.

The dandelion seed has a built-in parachute that lets it travel on the wind.

Wheee!

This dwarf mistletoe shoots out seeds like a cannon. Its seeds can travel as far as 50 feet [15.24 meters].

Whoah!!

The seeds of the maple tree are like miniature helicopters. As they fall, they twirl away from the parent plant.

Fruit attracts birds and mammals. They eat the fruit—and the seeds inside. The hard outer covering of the seeds protects the seed. The seeds pass through the animal and land and germinate in a new place.

Some seeds are sticky or have hooks. They take a ride on birds or mammals.

WHY DO PLANTS HAVE LIFE CYCLES?

Like all other living things, plants must make new plants to take their place when they die. Otherwise, they would become **extinct**.

The seeds from one plant grow into new plants which produce seeds of their own and so on and so on. Each plant produces the next generation.

An old tree crashes to the ground and starts to decay. Its rotting bark is home to a new tree. Because the old tree acts as a nursery for the new one, it is called a nurse log.

Dead plants are eaten by earthworms and insects and turn into rich soil for the next generation of plants. This earthworm eats its weight in rotting plants every day.

ENTERING RARE
WETLAND HABITAT
PRESERVE

Please stay on path to
avoid disturbing this
fragile habitat.
Remember, it is one
of the few places that
wetland species can
carry on their
life cycles.

The swamp pink, a wildflower that grows in wetlands, is endangered. Its seeds cannot find the right place to germinate because the wetlands where it lives are being drained.

DIFFERENT PLANT LIFE CYCLES

The life cycle of some plants lasts only a few weeks. Other plants have cycles that start in the spring and end in the fall. Some parent plants die after they have produced seeds. Others live on for many years. The time from germination to death is the plant's **life span**.

The radish is a whiz. If left in the ground, it will produce tiny flowers and seeds—all in just weeks.

Tomato seed   Radish seed

1 week   2 weeks   5 weeks   8 weeks

The bristlecone pine is an old timer. Its life span can last more than 4,000 years. During that time, it produces many generations of new plants.

Hello, old-timer!

Ferns do not have seeds. Instead they have **spores**. But they still have a life cycle. Their life cycle goes from spore to an in-between stage called a prothallus to new fern to spore.

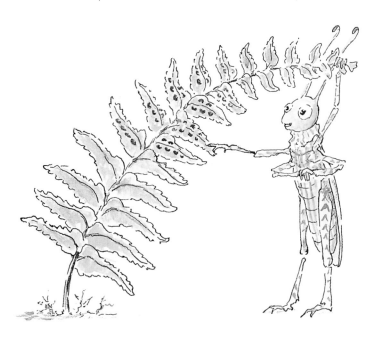

Spores are released from tiny brown sacs on the underside of the leaf. The spores float through the air to a new home.

Plant life cycles never stop. Round and round they go.

SEE A LIFE CYCLE

The life cycle of the pea takes 9 – 15 weeks. Plant one and you can watch its life cycle, from seed to plant to seed.

You will need:

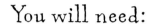

a nail

a paper cup

a saucer

potting soil

3 pea seeds

a calendar and pencil

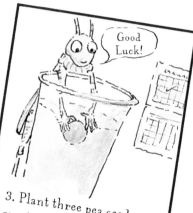

Good Luck!

3. Plant three pea seeds, spacing them evenly in the cup. Note the date of planting on a calendar.

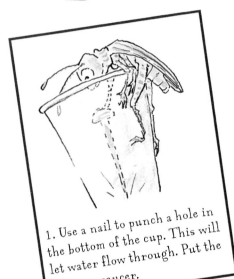

1. Use a nail to punch a hole in the bottom of the cup. This will let water flow through. Put the cup on a saucer.

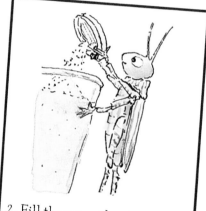

2. Fill the cup with potting soil.

grunt

4. Put the cup and saucer in a sunny spot. Water every two or three days.

Welcome! . . . gootchie goo!

5. When a seedling emerges, note the date on the calendar. How many days did it take for the first seed to germinate? Wait a few days. Pull out one seedling, leaving the two most healthy ones.

6. Watch as the seedlings become mature plants. On the calendar, note when the first flower forms. How many days did it take for the plant to flower?

7. Check the flowers every day. Watch for a pod to form. Watch what happens to the flower as the pod forms.

8. When the pod has stopped growing, remove it from the plant and split it open. Do you see the seeds inside? You may eat them.

9. Keep watering the parent plant and observing it. On the calendar, note when it starts to die. How long is the pea plant's life span?

MY LIFE
by
A. PLANT
What a great life!

GLOSSARY

anthers: the part of the flower that produces and holds the pollen. The anthers are at the end of a long filament. Together, anther and filament make up the stamen.

chlorophyll: the green coloring in leaves that helps with photosynthesis.

cross-pollination: when pollen from the anthers of one plant travels to the pistil of another plant.

extinct: no longer found in the wild. A species, or kind of plant, becomes extinct when there are no more of them.

flower: the blossom of a plant where seeds are produced. The flower contains the stamen and the pistil.

fruit: the enlarged ovary and seeds of a plant. Vegetable plants may have a part called a fruit.

germination: the sprouting of a seedling from a seed.

life cycle: the stages a plant goes through—from seed to plant to seed.

life span: the length of time from germination until the plant dies.

ovary: the part of pistil where seeds form.

photosynthesis: the process by which a plant uses the sun's energy to change water and the gas carbon dioxide into food for the plant. Through photosynthesis plants make their own food.

pistil: the part of the flower where the pollen must land in order for pollination to occur. The pistil is made up of the stigma, style, and ovary.

pollen: tiny dustlike particles that must travel from the anthers to the pistil in order for pollination to occur and seeds to form.

pollination: when pollen from the anthers travels to the pistil.

seed: a tiny, new plant with a food supply and outer covering.

seedling: a young plant.

self-pollination: when pollen travels from the anthers to the pistil of the same plant.

spores: the seedlike part of ferns, fungi, and some other plants.